IMAGES OF ENGLAND

DARLINGTON
REMEMBERED

VERA CHAPMAN

TEMPUS

Frontispiece: St Cuthbert's parish church gateway. This early 1960s drawing by the author shows how evergreens obscured the town's graveyard until landscaping in around 1970 opened it up as parkland.

First published 2005

Tempus Publishing Limited
The Mill, Brimscombe Port,
Stroud, Gloucestershire, GL5 2QG
www.tempus-publishing.com

British Library Cataloguing in Publication Data.
A catalogue record for this book is available from the British Library.

ISBN 0 7524 3555 8

Typesetting and origination by Tempus Publishing Limited.
Printed in Great Britain.

Contents

High Row and West Row looking towards Prospect Place and Northgate, *c.* 1906.

Introduction

I came to live in Darlington somewhat by chance. My husband's new job was on Teesside. We were to be shown some new housing on a tour starting from Thornaby station. Coming from Old Trafford and the heavy industrial zone along the Manchester Ship Canal in the foggiest winter I could remember, the prospect was not enticing! So we did our own explorations. The coast was bleak and treeless. Hedges leaned away from the sea. A Saltburn resident asserted that her washing would blow dry even on a wet day! We turned inland and from the A1 could see house building in progress across the Tees. Driving through white-painted suburbs with cared-for gardens we found that Bussey & Armstrong, Blacketts and Raine Brothers were building over Hummersknott Park, the largest of the old Quaker landscapes. Reuben Raine had just what we needed. So in June 1959, in a year of prolonged drought and heatwave, we moved into our white-painted house and started to create a garden out of clay soil baked like concrete. And then began our exploration of Darlington.

We took to the town straight away! A busy market town and shopping centre, it stands on the banks of the river Skerne near its confluence with the Tees, the historic boundary between Yorkshire and County Durham. This compact town of around 100,000 people is surrounded by beautiful countryside, rural villages with greens, a network of local roads and formerly a spider's web of railway branch lines centred on the town. Darlington stands astride the Great North Road of old – the A1 trunk road of today – and the east coast main line railway which all link London and Edinburgh. It also has an expanding regional airport nearby, recently renamed the Durham and Tees Valley Airport. Claiming to be the 'Birthplace of the Railways', the town did indeed launch in 1825 the world's first steam-hauled public railway, the Stockton and Darlington Railway, which ran from Shildon via Darlington to Stockton-on-Tees.

Now voted by the Civic Trust as one of the six best towns in which to live and work, Darlington's town centre, based on one of the country's largest marketplaces, is a conservation area in which Georgian, Victorian and Edwardian buildings blend in a harmonious variety with others both vernacular and modern. So far it has escaped the comprehensive redevelopments and tower blocks which have damaged some historic towns. Its leafy suburbs and tree-lined approach roads are a legacy of the villas, mansions and parklands of its Victorian prosperity.

We have inherited a town with a Saxon name (it first appeared in writing as 'Dearthingtun'), a pagan Saxon burial ground and traces of a Saxon church beneath our parish church. The Borough of Darlington was founded in the twelfth century by the Norman Bishop of Durham, Hugh de Puiset. He rebuilt the parish church of St Cuthbert in the new Early English Gothic style, and alongside it he also built his bishop's palace or manor house with a park beside the Skerne. His borough and his neighbouring Manor of Bondgate for his bond tenants were administered by a Bailiff of the Bishop's Borough until 1867. The twelfth-century pattern of streets, burgage plots or yards and the traditional street names – Row, Gate and Wynd – are still in use today.

Darlington seems to have had several periods of prosperity. In medieval times, the export of wool and the weaving, fulling and dyeing of woollen cloth were the mainstay of the Darlington economy. By the late fourteenth century, Darlington was by far the wealthiest of the Bishop's boroughs of Gateshead, Sunderland and Durham. In the sixteenth century leather was important, but it later gave way to a linen industry using the limy Skerne water for bleaching. In the eighteenth century shorthorn cattle and Teeswater sheep bred by local farmers brought fame and fortune when their fat beasts like the Ketton or Durham Ox, the Blackwell Ox and the celebrated bull Comet were paraded around the country. The local breed of shorthorn cattle was transformed into a pedigree breed which stocked the newly colonised lands of North and South America and Australia. The woollen industry survived, but linen became more important, organised as a cottage handloom industry, until two local men – Kendrew and Porthouse – invented and patented the first flax-spinning machine and set up three water-powered flax mills along the Skerne. In the nineteenth century, however, woollens revived when Edward Pease founded his Quaker family firm and dynasty in town, based at Priestgate Mill, Low Mill and Railway Mill, also along the Skerne.

The Quaker community, arriving in Darlington from the seventeenth century onward, engaged in shopkeeping, trade, industry and banking. In time they dominated local affairs and provided numerous mayors of the new municipal borough and a succession of MPs. Having moved into further industries – railways, coal and ironstone mining, coke, bricks, stone and water – they accumulated considerable wealth, built splendid houses and gardens and engaged in welfare and education.

The nineteenth century brought the prosperity of the railway age. In the 1860s the population of Darlington almost doubled and the town spread out beyond its medieval boundaries. The advent of the Stockton and Darlington Railway in 1825 sent terraced housing north to the first station and workshops and east to Bank Top and Albert Hill for the workers in the railway, iron and heavy engineering works in the Skerne valley. Villas and mansions were built in the west and south, but later became schools, hotels and offices or were demolished, their lands built over as residential suburbs. After two world wars, the 1960s railway closures and the loss of around 10,000 jobs came diversification and new, lighter industries on greenfield sites.

Darlington became a municipal borough in 1867 and a county borough in 1915. The outlying village of Cockerton came into the Borough in 1915, then Haughton le Skerne in 1930 and Blackwell in 1967. Darlington became a district of County Durham in 1974. It regained its independence as a unitary authority in 1997.

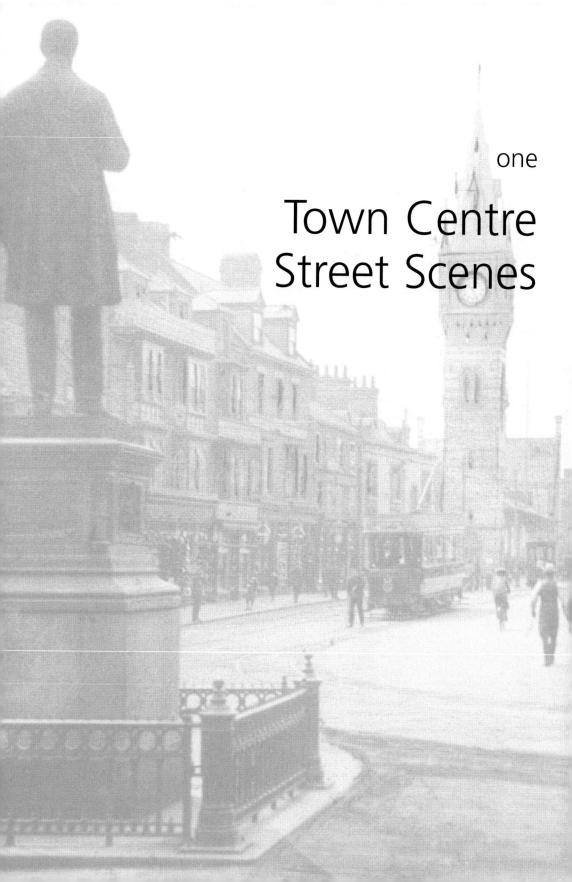

one

Town Centre Street Scenes

High Row from the south end. Georgian style premises extend as far as Post House Wynd, beyond which appear two banks of Edwardian and Victorian style, with the tall narrow, tile-fronted Art Nouveau premises of the architect J.P. Pritchett between. From the left can be distinguished, and remembered, John Grisdale's ladies' fashions and Taylor's Drug Company, a chemist's. Lipton's grocer's was on this row in the 1960s.

High Row from the north end. Looking from the left from Backhouses Bank are Georgian-style premises which include Singer's, selling sewing machines, Dunn & Sons, men's outfitters, Dresser & Sons, printers and binders, and Public Benefit Boot Company, boots and shoes. Joseph Pease's statue was moved up to avoid the tram lines, wires and general traffic at this busy road junction.

Above: A view from Prospect Place. On the left is
Prebend Row and the Town Clock, with the Town
Hall and Horsemarket in the distance. Pease's statue
was moved again in 1958, to the paved area at High
Row corner. This was the Great North Road of old°
and coaching inns and stables were a feature of the
town. In the 1960s cars used to queue in Grange
Road to get in and there was a Belisha beacon
crossing to get pedestrians across from High Row to
the Covered Market.

Right: High Row, formerly the Headrow, was
landscaped at the start of the twentieth century into
a three-level scheme with Shap granite steps and
balustraded recesses for seating. It gave a memorable
distinction and dignity to the town centre.

Prospect Place, where High Row ends. Bondgate curves off to Woodland Road and Cockerton whilst the curved tramlines lead past the London City & Midland Bank into Northgate, joining the straight ones from West Row and Prebend Row. The Midland Bank buildings of 1867 in Prospect Place were demolished in 1923 and rebuilt in 1926.

The tram is travelling along Northgate. Pease's statue stands in front of the North Eastern Insurance Company and the Yorkshire Bank and clearly shows its isolated position in the road junction.

Northgate House. Initially named Telegraph House this, the only high-rise building in Darlington, is an office block completed in 1977. Slow to let, it was not fully occupied until 1989. Renamed Northgate House, its top floor opened in 2003 as the aptly named Viewpoint Suite for conferences and training courses.

The old Technical College and Presbyterian church, Northgate. Designed by George Gordon Hoskins in red brick and orange terracotta, it opened in 1897. The grand staircase is in red sandstone. The distant spire rises from St George's Presbyterian church, designed by John Ross, 1867–69.

Above: Nurses' Home, Northgate. An imposing detached residential property opposite North Lodge Park gates, it stands next to the castellated Citadel of the Salvation Army. Its rear garden slopes down to the Skerne whose vale was formerly full of orchards. The house in recent years served as the Domestic Science Department of the old Technical College, Northgate and then as a restaurant.

Right: Tubwell Row. The lower part is named Stonebridge. The view is from St Cuthbert's Bridge, an iron bridge, which in 1895 replaced a three-arched stone bridge of 1767. This was the age-old crossing into town, with a ford, stepping stones and a causeway.

Post House Wynd was formerly named Glovers Wynd and Charegate. This narrow lane led from High Row to Skinnergate, the back lane behind the High Row burgage plots. The post house was at the front corner of the lane. Behind it was stabling. The Old Dun Cow inn is on the left of the picture.

Chancery Lane. Gardens of town houses developed in the eighteenth and nineteenth century as 'yards', crammed with dwellings, crafts and small workshops. Entrances to the old yards could be open tunnels, doorways or more ornate features, such as Chancery Lane leading off Horsemarket and through to Houndgate.

Russell's Yard, High Row. Demolished in the late 1960s, it was one of the last inhabited yards. Women residents were reluctant to leave, as it was so convenient to live in the town centre. The yards were floored in around 1900 with shiny blue scoriae blocks made from steelworks slag; these blocks were a characteristic of Darlington.

Clark's Yard, High Row. An awkward finkle or bend linked this yard to Skinnergate and corners of buildings were chamfered to ease carts through. This yard is now active with small businesses.

Bull Wynd, off Horsemarket. The old stone bull with a shovel-like tail is probably the crest of the Bulmer family who owned the corner burgage plot on the South Row of the Market Place. A Bull Inn was recorded here in 1613 and probably existed earlier. About 1660, the plot was bought by John Pease, a grocer, and in due course became the home of Edward Pease, 'Father of the Railways'.

Houndgate, 1973. The Bull burgage plot ran through to Houndgate as a walled garden in Edward Pease's time, and is now a small park. Houndgate became a fashionable residential area. Selby House, for a time a girl's school and forerunner of Polam Hall School, later became the Town Clerk's office and Registry office, the smaller building housing a solicitor's firm. The fountain, the top tier of a larger one at the top end of Tubwell Row and later in Green Park, was moved to Houndgate in 1970 on the centenary of the first publication in Darlington of the *Northern Echo*.

Edward Pease's house and Central Hall. The house was later the offices of Francis Mewburn, 'the world's first railway solicitor', and the legal brains behind the Stockton and Darlington Railway. When Darlington Historical Society was founded in the early 1960s, the premises were still packed from stone-floored cellar to attic with solicitors' old records, and the walled garden was derelict. The elegant Central Hall is dated MDCCCXLVI (1846) above the former main doorway in Bull Wynd. Designed by Darlington architect John Middleton, the Hall was the centre of nineteenth-century social life, meetings and events. Later it became a cinema and in the 1960s the town's rates office. Beautifully renovated by the Borough Council, it again hosts concerts, meetings and social events.

two

Market and Shops

An old Market Place scene, looking north-eastwards. The great Market Place originally bounded by High Row (Head Row), Tubwell Row, Horsemarket (South Row) and St Cuthbert's churchyard, is one of the largest in England.

Old Market Place scene, looking north-westwards. The Market Place was probably laid out in the twelfth century by Bishop Hugh de Puiset, when he built the church, the bishop's palace and his park beside the river Skerne.

Town Clock, Market Hall and the old Town Hall. Designed by Alfred Waterhouse, perhaps the most famous architect of Victorian England, it was completed in 1863. Commissioned by the town's Board of Health, its chairman, J.W. Pease, gave the Town Clock. The exterior shops on West Row were a later addition.

The Roman-style Market Cross is inscribed, 'Erected by Dame Dorothy Brown 1727'. She was a descendant of Richard Barnes, a sixteenth-century Bishop of Durham. It stood first at the top of Tubwell Row, then inside the Market Hall, then languished in the Council's store yard at Hundens. Given new steps and finial and a prominent new site, it was the first stage of the Market Place refurbishment of the 1990s.

COVERED MARKET, DECEMBER 1973. *Vera Chapman* '76
before refurbishment.

Market Hall interior, 1973. A great variety of goods are still sold, especially by butchers, greengrocers and confectioners. Small items of clothing and hardware are also popular.

Murray's central bakery and confectionery stall served in the Market Hall many years. The family had their own local bakery and eventually spawned about a dozen shops in the district.

Right: The Market Hall is usually called the Covered Market. Being of cast iron and glass construction, it is well lit by high windows as this view of one of the long aisles shows.

Below: Harrison's butcher's were the best dressed stall in Empire Week, 1932. The family firm dates from 1799. It had a shop in Park Street with an abattoir behind in Valley Street, and there were other shops, too. In time, a Harrison daughter married a Manson but the business remained under the Harrison name until this year, 2005, when Don Manson retired. It is now renamed Hannigan's, for its new owner.

The Market Square from the new Town Hall forecourt, *c.* 1970. On the left is the corner where outdoor market stall frames were stored and where the old deanery once stood, while on the right is Bakehouse Hill corner. In between, the long high-up windows of the Market Hall are visible. The glass veranda has since been renewed. The sculpture 'Resurgence' is in the foreground.

The Market Square, 1993. Before refurbishment, the Market Square was for most of the time a car park. The Market Cross is in its new position, and the renewed glass veranda is on the left.

Laying setts at Feethams, 1996. A new raised pedestrian crossing to the Town Hall entrance was emphasised by railway lines, with flat granite slabs to walk on and, for traffic, strips of warning setts and a bump!

An archaeological dig in 1994. Prior to the Market Place refurbishment thirty-two medieval skeletons were unearthed in shallow graves in front of St Cuthbert's churchyard wall.

Reburial ring 1995. In the cavities of the enlarged driving wheel of Locomotion are interred the remains of those thirty-two inhabitants of medieval Darlington. The true size of the Locomotion engine's wheel can be seen on page 90.

The refurbished Market Place from the churchyard gates. The refurbishment scheme incorporated local history themes. For a 'railway town' the locomotion wheel motif is used on bench ends, brackets for hanging flower baskets, lamp posts and bus shelters. The whole Market Place is floored with Shap granite flags recalling the numerous boulders of this rock left locally after the Ice Age, such as Bulmer's Stone in Northgate, and the Taylor Manson memorial stone in South Park.

Charles Henry Sharp's pawnshop, East Row, Market Place. The pledge shop was down a side passage on the left. The three golden balls, a pawnbrokers' sign descended from the symbol of the Medici family, powerful merchants in Renaissance Florence, projects from the roof's balustrade. These ornate premises in Renaissance style were designed by G.G. Hoskins and built by Ian R. Mackenzie in red brick and terracotta, *c.* 1897.

Old style shopfronts, Horsemarket, 1974. Several properties in a poor state were demolished at the back and rebuilt whilst the listed fronts were propped up intact and saved.

John Lear & Sons, ironmongery and hardware, Horsemarket, 1965. This long narrow shop next to Chancery Lane was a traditional country-town ironmonger pre-dating DIY superstores. Small quantities could be bought loose and practical advice on use given. Long wooden counters stretched back culminating in a central staircase and a long-case clock.

The School Furnishing Company ('Furni' for short!) This ornate building on the Skinnergate-Coniscliffe Road corner, also designed by Hoskins and built by Mackenzie, opened on 22 June 1897, Queen Victoria's Diamond Jubilee Day. It supplied classroom furniture and school stationery, and was closely linked with John Pease and the Religious Tract Bible Society.

High Row, south end, 1965. This close-up shows more clearly some well-known traders, but not all have survived.

Above: The King's Head hotel, Northgate. An old coaching inn here on the Great North Road was rebuilt in 1900 by Mackenzie to the red brick Renaissance design of Hoskins who adopted this style for many of his town buildings. The ground floor frontage comprised two rows of shops and the entrances to the hotel and to extensive stables.

Right: Todd Brothers, drapers, Crown Street (for sale in 1982). In 1901-02 they extended round the corner from Northgate into the newly constructed Crown Street. Their new style building with its shiny brown faience tiled frontage comprised showrooms, workrooms, a household furnishing department and a house. Now a listed building, it served as Emma Harte's shopping emporium during filming in 1983 of Barbara Taylor Bradford's 1980 novel *A Woman of Substance.*

Opposite: Bakehouse Hill corner, 1982. The Quaker family grocer and tea dealer Thomas Pease, Son & Co. traded at this site on Bakehouse Hill corner in the Market Place through five generations, ending in 1981. Thomas's descendants expanded as wholesale and retail wine and spirits merchants with an extensive trade in Britain and overseas. Their prominent new premises of 1900 in bright red and orange brick were designed by architect J.P. Pritchett Jr based at High Row, better known for his churches. Recently restored, it significantly enhances the conservation area in the town centre.

North Star newspaper offices and printworks, Crown Street-Quebec Street corner. Designed by G.G. Hoskins, the front in the 1960s was Snowball's ladies fashions and is now a greengrocery.

Darlington Co-operative Industrial Society Ltd, Branch No. 6, Victoria Road, built in 1903. The Society was founded in 1868. New central premises, Darneton House, were opened in 1931 in Priestgate and ran as a department store through to Tubwell Row in 1964. It was recently demolished to make way for the Cornmill Shopping Centre. The Co-op had numerous branches in the town, suburbs and region.

George Miller, Bacon Factor, Darlington. Bringing home the bacon or delivering it? This photograph of 1885 was given to the author by Mrs Moira Beswick. Her grandfather, Thomas Neilson Miller, is the young lad. We have not identified the house.

Harrison's Park Street shop. One of several shops allied to their Covered Market stall (see also page 23). Two framed photographs were kept on display on the stall and are copied courtesy of Don Manson.

Above: Skinnergate shops. The street has retained a traditional variety of small businesses. Zissler's also had a pork butchers in Bondgate. They may have been one of the many German families who settled in the North East after the First World War continuing the old Baltic trade links.

Left: George Wildsmith & Sons, Grocers and Provision Merchants at 12 Skinnergate, were established in 1867 and, after three generations there, closed on 24 February 1979. Their aromas of coffee, tea, cheeses and bacon wafted across Skinnergate to join the perfumes from Pressland's hairdressers!

Opposite, below: Goldfinch Wines. This general shop in Larchfield Street really was a corner shop. It served especially the customers in the small terraced houses in nearby streets such as Powlett Street and Raby Street, built when the Duke of Cleveland's estate west of Skinnergate was released for development in the 1870s.

Above: Charles Knott & Son. In this brush and paint store at the corner of Duke Street and Raby Terrace paints could be mixed to customers' specifications, a notable service to DIY.

Proud's hardware shop, 1974. On the corner of Northgate and Leadenhall Street, this brightly painted shop could hardly be missed. At the bottom end of the street St Luke's, stood a small English church of 1883 designed by J.P. Pritchett.

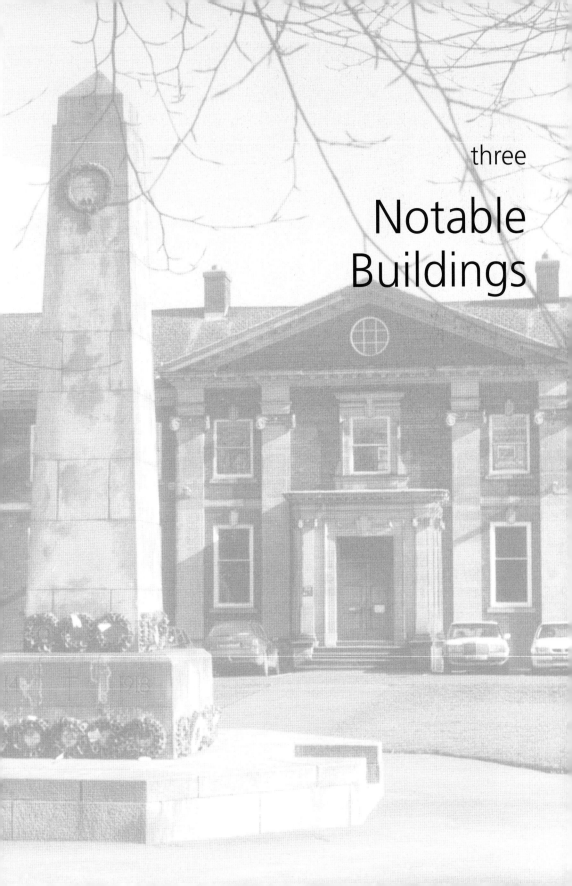

three

Notable
Buildings

A fragment of Tudor wall. This wall of handmade brick in Church Lane behind the Nag's Head is the sole survivor of the Great Fire of Darlington on 7 May 1585 in which some 273 homes were burned and 800 people made homeless. With water scarce due to a drought people unsuccessfully tried to douse the flames with milk and beer. A huge swathe of the upper town around High Row and Skinnergate was destroyed. A long period of neglect followed.

Doric House. A unique iron-framed building of 1860 in Tubwell Row with four round dormer windows and a two-slope mansard roof. The main windows are supported on cast iron brackets and exposed columns. The door and windows on the right light a spiral staircase. This is a Grade II listed building.

Barclays Bank, High Row, also a Grade II*
listed building. Designed as Backhouse's Bank
by Alfred Waterhouse with G.G. Hoskins as
clerk of the works, with Richardson as builder,
this building was completed in 1864. It is one
of the few stone buildings in town.

Barclays Bank doorway. Backhouse & Co.,
founded in 1774, was one of the many private
banks which amalgamated in 1896 to form
Barclay & Co. Ltd. The Backhouses used to be
linen and worsted manufacturers. Their first
bank was in Northgate, and they moved to a
site on High Row in 1815.

West Cemetery entrance gates and lodge. James Piggott Pritchett Jr designed the cemetery and two Early English mortuary chapels linked by an arch with a 107 foot spire. Completed in 1857 with twenty acres, it has twice been extended. Its crematorium was the first to be built in the Tees area. The considerable diversity of mature trees make it a virtual nature reserve.

Teacher Training College, Vane Terrace, 1960s. The women's training college was built for the British and Foreign Schools Society to train teachers for non-conformist schools. The simple Gothic style in smooth red brick was the design of J.P. Pritchett Jr, and was completed in 1875. The Arthur Pease Practice School was added later. The college was closed in 1970 in a spate of government closures and in 1979 became the Arts Centre.

The original part of the Edward Pease Free Library. Edward Pease of Greencroft West died in 1880 leaving an endowment for education. The library in G.G. Hoskins' red brick Renaissance style was opened in 1885 by Edward's daughter Viscountess Lymington and extended in the same style in 1933.

Florence Street Almshouses. The six houses off Yarm Road at Bank Top were built in the early eighteenth century by the Bellasses Charity. Three pairs of twin Gothic porches gave entry. They were demolished during the 1960s or 1970s.

St Cuthbert's Home for Girls, Cleveland Avenue, late 1920s. The photograph was given to the author by Stephen Whitwell, who called the home the 'Waifs and Strays'! It opened in 1843 and could house up to forty girls until its closure in 1947. It reopened as St Cuthbert's Nursery between 1949 and 1972. Blocks of brick flats now stand on the site.

Sir E.D. Walker Homes, Coniscliffe Road. Walker was a lessee of NER bookstalls and refreshment rooms and founder of E.D. Walker & Wilson, one of the largest provincial newspaper distributors and wholesale newsagents and stationers. He was three times mayor, knighted in 1908 and died in 1919 leaving a bequest for homes for the aged. The thirty-six homes facing a large square green, with an assembly hall, superintendent's and nurse-matron's quarters, were designed by architect Joshua Clayton, built by Blackett & Son and opened in 1928.

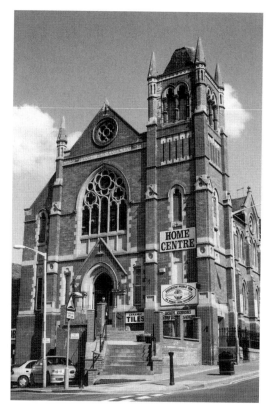

Right: Victoria Road Methodist New Connexion church. Built in 1883 on the corner of Hargreave Terrace, this outstanding decorated red brick Love Memorial Chapel was designed by A.H. Goodall of Nottingham. It seated 850 and had a Sunday school in the basement for 450. In the 1960s it was a wood warehouse (where useful offcuts could be had!) and has developed as a home improvement centre for bathrooms and kitchens.

Below: Old Technical College, Northgate. This G.G. Hoskins design built by Ian R. Mackenzie in 1894–97 is in Perpendicular style with quiet brickwork and orange terracotta dressings. It is Grade II listed. The Tudor-arched entrance under the tower leads to a grand ceremonial staircase in red sandstone.

Above: Greenbank Hospital. Another Hoskins design built by Mackenzie, it replaced a dispensary in the Market Hall and a small hospital in Russell Street, later the Conservative Club. Opened in December 1884 with flags and lanterns and a conversazione for 500 guests and the mayor, it depended on voluntary fund-raising and contributions. Initially for sixteen beds it was extended in 1895 and 1902, and remained in use until demolished when the later Memorial Hospital's new block was ready.

Left: Darlington Memorial Hospital and Cenotaph. The Memorial Hall and Porch were erected to the memory of Roland Boys Bradford VC, MC, of the Durham Light Infantry, the youngest Brigadier-General of the British Army, killed at the age of twenty-five at the battle of Cambrai in 1917, one of Darlington's four heroic Bradford brothers of the First World War.

Cassy M. Harker, hospital matron. She was the last matron of Darlington Memorial Hospital, and possibly the last in the whole of the NHS. She trained at Leeds General Infirmary, served at Mansfield as theatre sister, then again at Leeds as theatre superintendent dealing with war injuries. Matron at Chester and the Friarage, Northallerton, she later became matron at Darlington in 1962 with 300 nurses and 600 beds. When she retired in 1974 there were over 700 nurses and nearly 1,000 beds, but matrons had become a vanished species.

Kenneth C. McKeown, CBE, surgeon. Ken McKeown trained as a doctor at Queen's in Belfast, and after the Second World War his career peaked at Darlington District Hospital. He had served as an army surgeon during the battle of Britain, the London Blitz and the Normandy landings, the V2 rockets and RAF bomber casualties, and served later in Greece, Egypt and the Suez Canal Zone. Post-war changes from Cottage and Memorial Hospitals to the NHS gave him the opportunity to develop Darlington as a District General Hospital, and personally his expertise as a specialist in cancer of the oesophagus (gullet). He was a motivator for the establishment of St Teresa's Hospice at The Woodlands, Darlington.

Left: Darlington Civic Theatre, Parkgate. Formerly it was the New Hippodrome and Palace of Varieties designed by Hoskins in red brick and orange terracotta. It opened in 1907 and seated 1210. Saved from demolition by Darlington Operatic Society, it was bought by Darlington Borough Council in 1964 and preserved, restored and refurbished in 1990 with grant aid from the European Regional Development Fund to seat, refresh and entertain 900 in comfort. The gold, white and crimson auditorium is an Edwardian gem.

Below: Civic Theatre directors Brian Goddard, Andrew Jowett, Peter Todd and William McDonald at a party held by the Friends of the Theatre on 28 January 1990 to celebrate its success and look forward to the reopening of the theatre gallery and the building of bar facilities in a new extension.

Theatre Circle Bar. A gift of the Friends, it is here in action at the 'End of an Era' party in 1990. The bones of the dog of the first theatre owner, Signor Pepi, were found during construction.

The Quakers or Friends Meeting House, Skinnergate. On this site from the seventeenth century, it evolved in stages. Meeting houses for men and women were built at the rear and replaced in the nineteenth century by one larger room, soon to be followed by the present two-storied front rooms with the classical facade of 1840. The Meeting House could seat about 1000 in the 1890s. Joshua Sparkes had some part in the design of this Grade II listed building.

Above: Mechanics' Institution, Skinnergate. This has been attributed to Joseph M. Sparkes, 1853. The corner brickwork suggests that a classical façade was added to a plainer building. This educational centre for workers had a large assembly hall and meeting rooms for arts and science classes. It was later used as a theatre.

Left: The chairman's chair. Among the Institute's chairmen who used it would be Joseph Pease and Henry Pease.

Opposite, above: Upper storey façade, Bondgate. The Art Nouveau display appears to be an addition to an older building. Behind it is a room panelled in 1900, formerly Laverick's Coffee Room. The premises are now a branch of the Nationwide Building Society.

Binns' department store. Binns' of Sunderland set up in Darlington at this corner in 1922. After a serious fire in 1925 the store was rebuilt and gradually extended along High Row and Blackwellgate and reaching backwards to Mechanics' Yard. A unifying façade was adopted and in the 1960s the premises of a former branch of Boots the Chemist were incorporated. Ladies regret the closing of the Food Hall at the Blackwellgate end where delicious and unusual items were stocked.

Left: Prudentia. A statue of Prudence was displayed on all the Prudential Assurance Company's branches. This one was above the Northgate branch doorway and was transferred to the central escalator area of the new Cornmill Shopping Centre. In the 1960s, by contrast with the Cornmill, there were several small department stores in town: Doggarts, Lucks, Bainbridge Barkers, the Co-op and Todd Brothers. *(Photograph courtesy of Mike Hein-Hartmann.)*

Below: Cornmill Centre, Tubwell Row entrance, 1996. The stripe pattern of two-colour brickwork is reminiscent of Doggarts and of the old Technical College. The Centre was officially opened on 28 August 1992 by the Mayor David Lyonette accompanied by the Mayoress Mrs Carol Lyonette, and John Bywater, managing director of Burton Property Trust.

four

Terraces, Villas and Mansions

Left and below: Georgian terraced houses. On Coniscliffe Road near Cleveland Terrace corner are several attractive short terraces which mark the beginning of the town's suburban expansion westwards. A short terrace on the south side of the road backs on to Green Park, once part of the grounds of Joseph Pease's Southend mansion.

Victoria Road in 1963. This end-of-terrace at Feethams west corner was demolished to allow
St Cuthbert's Way inner ring road at Victoria Bridge to enter Victoria Road which was then
converted into a dual carriageway. The Skerne and bridge are now under the large roundabout.
The projecting sign indicated the Victoria Grill and Restaurant.

Pensbury Street, Bank Top. Terraced housing convenient for railway and industrial workers came
in the 1870s. This terrace opened behind on to a back lane parallel with the station platform and
sidings. Hargreave Terrace ran behind on the other side, its graceful curve reflecting the boundary
between the Bishop's High and Low Parks east of the Skerne.

An Edwardian Terrace. It stands on Coniscliffe Road between Beechwood Avenue and Oakdene Avenue and was probably built in the early 1900s.

Southend Avenue. A row of ten houses built in 1904 by Thomas Thornton between Beechwood Avenue and Oakdene Avenue. They faced the Crocus Walk wood, formerly the shelterbelt along Grange Road bordering the grounds of Joseph Pease's mansion Southend.

Art Nouveau-style housing, Cleveland Terrace. This new early twentieth century style in white pebbledash and locally with diamond-shaped motifs came into Darlington in single premises but probably influenced whole estates in the town in the 1930s.

The Mead, Yarm Road. Darlington's Garden City began to be built in 1912 on the White Farm estate opposite Cobden Street tram terminus, and later came The Fairway. Richardson's did most of the building. Privet hedges and grass verges with trees were the rule. At the time, a popular song was current in Darlington to a jaunty tune: 'In our little garden subbub, far away from the noise and hubbub…!'

Salutation Road. This long road was built in the 1930s on Salutation Farm land. The farmhouse stood at the corner of Coniscliffe Road and Carmel Road North. The tree-lined grass verges carried on the Garden City ideal, the national, post-war suburban dream.

Blackwell Village, a watercolour by local artist A.B. Dresser, *c.* 1912. It shows the smithy and cottage on the village green, the Punch Bowl Inn and farm on the right and the parkland wall of Blackwell Grange on the left.

Right: Westbrook, 1865. These semi-detached dwellings in polychrome brick beside the Cocker Beck near North Road Station were designed by G.G. Hoskins for young Henry Pease. In the early days of the Stockton and Darlington Railway the site had been sidings and coal drops. Henry developed a garden there.

Below: The Knoll, 1871. A G.G. Hoskins villa design in red brick at Linden Avenue corner for William Russell, ironmonger and plumber in business at 24 Blackwellgate.

Girls Training Home, Elton Parade. The building was designed by G.G. Hoskins in 1875, and from 1878 housed a school founded by Mary Ann Pease (later Mrs Hodgkin) of Elm Ridge for training twenty poor girls for good and useful service, to which they were sent out aged twenty-one. It was maintained at her expense. There was a house each for teacher and matron. Later it was for many years the Hygienic Laundry which closed around 1950. The building subsequently became flats, Welbeck House.

Darlington Grammar School, Vane Terrace, by G.G. Hoskins 1875. Founded as the Free Grammar School of Queen Elizabeth by a charter of 1563, it moved to this new site in 1878 opposite Stanhope Green, which was to be planted out as Stanhope Park. The headmaster's house is on the end, right, and the assembly hall above an undercroft playground on the left. About twenty pupils were boarded in the times of Headmasters Wood and Taylor. The school was much enlarged after the war, and is now Darlington Sixth Form College.

Nestfield Methodist Free Chapel and School, Albert Hill. This was a G.G. Hoskins design for R.H. Allan of Blackwell Grange, on whose Nestfield Farm the chapel was built. The chapel seated 500, no doubt from the nearby ironworks families. A plaque is dated 1867.

North Cemetery Chapels, Harrowgate Hill. The new cemetery designed by G.G. Hoskins with its two mortuary chapels was opened in 1874. Much of the cost was defrayed by members of the Pease family in memory of their father Joseph who died in 1872.

Above: Stanhope Road villas. At the corner of Stanhope Road and Abbey Road a striking group of houses with Dutch gables were built by Ian R. MacKenzie. One is a veterinary practice, another was a doctors' group practice until 2004.

Left: Wilkin Drewery's Villa, 1903, at Abbey Road and Cleveland Avenue corner was also built by Ian R. MacKenzie. It is now a day nursery. Wilkin Drewery owned an old style grocery business near the town end of Coniscliffe Road. On retirement, the handsome shop fittings were taken to Beamish North of England Museum. The photograph was taken after snow.

Opposite below: The Woodlands, Woodland Road. It began as a small villa built in 1815 by Robert Botcherby, a local timber merchant. Joseph Whitwell Pease, the eldest son of Joseph Pease of Southend married in 1854 and made The Woodlands his first home. In 1860 builders Richardson and Ross almost doubled its size and added the tower and bay, nurseries and service rooms. Joseph's interests were the NER and the Tees Conservancy. He served thirty-five years as MP for South Durham and Barnard Castle, accepting a knighthood in 1882. He had already left for his new home in Cleveland. After several other occupants The Woodlands became St Teresa's Hospice in 1999.

Blackwell Grange. The first George Allan, a general merchant, acquired the Blackwell estate in 1693. The central part is the old house which he enlarged in 1710. The wing on the left he built for the marriage of his son with local heiress Thomasine Prescott. The matching wing on the right was added by Sir Henry Marshman Havelock Allan in 1889. Bought by Darlington Corporation in 1955, it became an annex to the old Technical College, and from 1970 a hotel. Elegant rooms, grand staircase, family portraits and a mature lime avenue are among its historic attractions.

Southend. Edward Backhouse, a banker, built a small plain villa on land beside Grange Road. He moved to Sunderland around 1820. Joseph Pease, a merchant, renamed it 'Southend' and extended the house to three storeys, with a fine portico and large bays and summerhouses, and the garden to twenty-seven acres. A hidden staircase took servants unobtrusively about their work. It later became a Roman Catholic girls' school, then the Grange Hotel and, after renovation, reopened in 1998 as the New Grange Hotel.

The public life panel from the Joseph Pease statue, representing his political and business associates. He was chairman of Joseph Pease & Partners, the family business, treasurer and extender of the Stockton and Darlington Railway, and had interests in collieries, engineering, steam ploughing, Middlesbrough new town, education and the anti-slavery movement. His gifts included the Town Clock, roadside drinking fountains and schools in colliery villages.

Right: The life-size statue of Joseph Pease, dressed in the Quaker garb of the time, was erected by public subscription and unveiled on 27 September 1875, the Golden Jubilee of the Stockton and Darlington Railway. The massive pedestal of Peterhead granite bears four bronze bas-relief panels representing some of his concerns: elections, a colliery school, a colliery engine and docks, and black slaves.

Below: West Lodge, West Crescent. A small villa was built in the late eighteenth century by James Backhouse, a linen maker who together with his sons Jonathan and James founded Backhouse's Bank in 1774. After his death his nephew Thomas retired to Darlington and around 1903 built this new front pediment and pyramidal side pavilions. From the mid-nineteenth century it was the home of Sir David Dale, with interests in industry, mining, railways and a pioneer of social reform. The Wood family shown here were more recent residents between the wars. The grounds were built over and one of the West Crescent houses is visible in the background.

Above: Larchfield. This villa on Coniscliffe Road was built by John Backhouse, a banker and son of Jonathan of West Lodge. A keystone over the rear door was inscribed 'IEB 1811'. At first it was named Lamb Flatt House, a field name, but by the 1820s it was Paradise. The right end and turret are an addition. Francis Mewburn, who was the first railway solicitor and last Bailiff of the Bishop's Borough, renamed it Larchfield, reputedly saying that no solicitor should live in paradise. Later it became a Roman Catholic girl's school, and more recently was demolished to build a church hall.

Left: Pierremont clock tower, Tower Road. John Botcherby built a Gothic villa in the 1830s near the Cocker Beck. By the middle of the century it belonged to Henry Pease, who greatly enlarged it. In 1873 Alfred Waterhouse designed additions: a business room, domestic quarters, a conservatory, fernery and sunken walk and the clock tower and entrance arch. From 1864 beyond Woodland Road he created Pierremont Gardens with an entrance lodge, lake with boat cave, grotto and waterfall, fruit garden, kitchen garden, a rose-arcaded promenade and the handsome fountain now in South Park (see page 75).

Brinkburn. About a third of the south front is shown here of the splendid mansion built behind Pierremont for Henry Pease's eldest son Henry Fell Pease. Designed by John Ross, it was completed in 1862 in Pease's cream coloured brick with red sandstone dressings. The large drawing-room ballroom had marble pillars. The mansion was demolished in stages but the stables block survives as offices. The grounds became a park but the 1873 entrance lodge was recently demolished.

Elm Ridge south front, Blackwell, 1974. John Pease of East Mount provided two mansions at Salutation crossroads for his daughters: Elm Ridge for Mary Anna and Woodburn for Sophia. Both were designed by G.G. Hoskins and built in stone in similar styles. Woodburn was demolished, but some of its stone motifs and building blocks enhance the local 1930s houses. Mary Anna married J.B. Hodgkin and lived at Elm Ridge for over fifty years. She died in the late 1920s, whereupon it became Elm Ridge Methodist church with the exterior unchanged.

Left: Greencroft East. The huge Gothic pile in cream brick, with red sandstone dressings was built around 1860 as semi-detached houses for Edward Pease and Gurney Pease, sons of Joseph Pease. Later it was divided into three dwellings. Eventually the west and centre were demolished, and Northumbria Water for a time occupied the east end, now also gone.

Below: Blackwell Hill, *c.* 1873. Eliza Backhouse married Robert Barclay and they built their mansion on the high bank above the Tees near Blackwell Bridge overlooking north Yorkshire. It was designed by John Ross. It was demolished around 1970 and the neo-Georgian houses of Farr Holme were built.

Mowden Hall, Barnes Road. John Beaumont Pease of North Lodge bought the Bushel Hill Farm estate. His son Edwin Lucas Pease demolished the house in the 1870s and built Mowden Hall, variously attributed to architects John Ross, Richardson and Ross, and Alfred Waterhouse. The latter did alterations in 1881-85 and 1899. The Hall was a new departure in style, in bright red brick with red sandstone dressings, red tiled roofs and featuring red terracotta sunflower heads. It has had various functions over the years including a school, an army headquarters, an egg-packing station and an industrial firm's offices, followed by the Department of Education and Science with a new office block alongside from 1970.

Thornfield, Thornfield Road. This red brick mansion of Gothic flavour perched on a steep hillock above Carmel Road North was built for John Marley, a mining and civil engineer who was exploring and proving the ironstone resources of the Cleveland Hills. With John Vaughan he discovered the ironstone outcrop above Eston Hill. A datestone on the main doorway reads 'JSM 1859'. The mansion is now subdivided and enclosed by a circular road with a ring of semi-detached houses on the outer side, some by J.P. Pritchett.

Left: Grantley, Carmel Road North. This modern-looking villa was built in 1899 for G.N. Watson, solicitor. It was designed by G.G. Hoskins who characteristically produced long exterior reeded chimney stacks. Its red brick and red tile construction kept it looking modern during many years as offices, but it has just been demolished and small new houses now occupy its site.

Below: Pilmore Hall, Hurworth on Tees was designed by Alfred Waterhouse and built for banker Alfred Backhouse in 1863. It was this project that brought G.G. Hoskins to Darlington as clerk of the works, after which he pursued his career of architect to prolific effect in the region. In the early twentieth century the estate switched names to Rockcliffe and after the Second World War was the site of the St John of God Hospital for tuberculosis patients, later becoming the St Cuthbert's Hospital, specialising in orthopaedic care. In 1996 much of the estate was sold to Middlesbrough Football Club for use as a training ground.

five

Water
Features

Above: Tees Cottage Pumping Station and Steam Museum. A gas and water company was formed in 1849. Two beam engines lifted water from the Tees, one to depositing tanks and filter beds, the other to service reservoirs at Bushel Hill and Harrowgate Hill. Tees water is softer than the town's well water. A 1904 beam engine, the rare 1914 gas-powered engine and the 1926 electric pump house operate on some weekends to show the history of water supply in Darlington.

Left: The Tub Well was one of three public wells in the town centre, covered over in 1886 because it was too polluted, but rediscovered during the building of the Cornmill Centre. On the official opening day of the Centre, 18 August 1992, the Mayor, Councillor David Lyonette, unveiled the water pump that now marks the location of the Tub Well.

Right: Drinking fountain, 1974, constructed in 1866, Carmel Road North. Mounted on the wall near the gateway into Arthur Peases's Hummersknott Park, this cast iron fountain was probably removed when Hummersknott Avenue was being built in the 1950s. Seven drinking fountains of varied designs were gifted to the town by Joseph Pease. A small plain one is on a wall by the South Park showground, but the freestanding one on the approach road to North Road station has gone.

Below: Another drinking fountain from 1866, this time in Milbank Road. This cast iron drinking fountain is on the park wall of The Woodlands, where Joseph Whitwell Pease formerly lived.

Southend drinking fountain, once again from 1866, in Coniscliffe Road. This fountain is on the wall of Joseph Pease's Southend grounds, the only brick fountain and one of the few with a small animal basin. Note the dove of peace in the keystone.

Grange Road drinking fountain built of stone and set into the stone wall of Joseph Pease's Southend park wall outside the Crocus Walk in Southend Avenue. Note again the dove of peace, with a pea pod in its beak, a pun on the family name.

Right: Memorial drinking fountain, Hurworth. 'Erected by Alice Maude Scurfield to commemorate the accession of HM George V, 1911'. The drinking bowl is of Shap granite. There is a tap housing nearby. The Scurfield family lived at Hurworth House, now a preparatory school.

Below: A trough at Blands Corner roundabout, Blackwell. Inscribed 'Drinking Fountain and Cattle Trough Association, 70 Victoria Street, SW', it was moved to a less vulnerable position on the grass verge when the southern bypass was built.

North Lodge Park fountain. An ornamental cast iron fountain in the former grounds of Elmfield, North Road, the home of the Kitching family, iron founders and railway engine builders.

Fountain in Houndgate. Erected first in 1858 in Tubwell Row and later in Green Park, Oakdene Avenue, this ornamental fountain was moved to Houndgate in 1970 on the centenary of the first publication in Darlington of the *Northern Echo*. It has a cast iron bowl on a carved stone plinth.

The Pierremont fountain, South Park. Formerly the centrepiece of Henry Pease's new Pierremont South Gardens, created in 1864, it was re-erected in the town's South Park when Henry's gardens were built over. This spectacular terracotta fountain had twenty-one jets. The main basin was surrounded by specially-designed vases and crescent-shaped flower beds. Grade II listed, it is to be restored in the South Park restoration project.

South Park lake. This Edwardian postcard shows the lake, virtually a widening of the river Skerne below Park House. Swags of flowering plants can just be seen above the upper terrace path. Topical designs are still created each summer.

South Park boating lake and landing stage. After wartime neglect it was by 1959 a morass, but it has since been reclaimed as grassland and river and is soon to be part of the South Park restoration.

North Lodge Park boat cave and lake. This popular viewpoint of the park shows the former grounds of John Beaumont Pease's North Lodge villa. In 1901 Darlington Borough Council developed this remnant into a public park, with water for the lake to be supplied by the outflow from the town's nearby swimming baths! There was skating in cold Edwardian winters. In 1932 the lake was filled in and in 1954 the boathouse was demolished.

Brinkburn Dene. Land along the Cocker Beck valley was acquired by the Borough Council in 1912. Before the war it was partly allotment gardens. After the war it was transformed into a park to create employment. Opened in 1925 by the mayor W.E. Pease, it still abounds in spring flowers and seventy species of birds. Owls, woodpeckers, kingfishers, bats and grey squirrels may be seen. Below Pierremont's shady bank Henry Pease formerly had an ice house. Native British trees were planted and a few conifers.

On the Tees near Blackwell in 1970, a canoe constructed from a ready-to-assemble kit is given its first trial.

Hell Kettles, near Hurworth Place. Members of Darlington and Teesdale Naturalists' Field Club are pond-dipping in 1964, with permission. Tradition tells that the earth 'burst forth on Christmas Day 1179AD' leaving several sulphurous pools. Legends abound, but the pools were probably due to the dissolution of soluble layers in the underlying dolomitic limestone.

The New Spa at Croft Spa. The old spa was discovered in the seventeenth century. The new well was drilled in 1827 and this pump room and suite of hot and cold baths and a hotel were built with an assembly ballroom. Liver, kidney and skin complaints and rheumatism were treated. The spa itself survived on a small scale until the Second World War.

Gainford Spa. This was discovered during boring for coal on the Tees bank. It led to the building of small boarding houses in the village, but did not develop further. The old bowl-like font was recently damaged, but a similar one replaces it.

Dinsdale Spa. In 1789 sulphurous water burst forth during boring for coal on the Tees bank near Middleton St George. A succession of bath houses followed, and a large would-be hotel on the cliff above, culminating in this small hotel and baths in 1880. In 1910 it became Dinsdale Golf Club House, which in 1983 was divided into dwellings. The large seventy bedroom hotel became in turn a retreat, a boarding school and a nursing home.

An old painting of Great Burdon Mill on the rural Skerne.

The urban Skerne between the new Town Hall and St Cuthbert's Way inner ring road. The name Skerne means 'bright waters'. It used to support twelve species of fish, including trout, and was once famed for eels and pike. In 1810 it was powering twelve watermills.

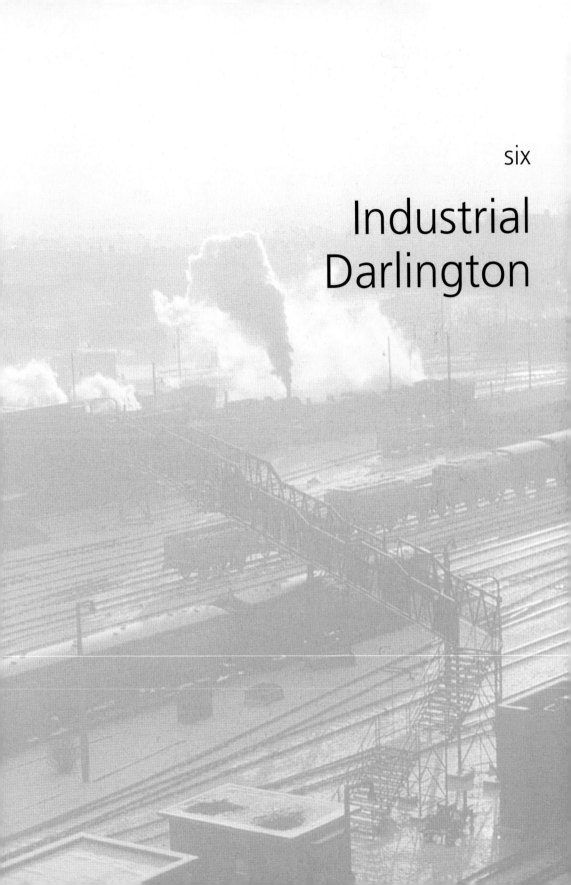

six

Industrial
Darlington

Left: Floreat Industria – 'Let industry flourish'. An old coat of arms on a gateway pillar at the entrance to the Crocus Walk in Southend Avenue. It was believed to be unofficial; the recently, officially registered coat of arms bears the motto Optima Petamus – 'Let us seek the best'.

Below: Potts Memorial. The clock stage added in 1901 on to Park House in South Park and a plaque above its doorway are a memorial to William Potts (1809-1887), a clockmaker of Darlington and Leeds. Like his father, he trained as a clockmaker in Darlington and from 1832 set up in Leeds a thriving business making large-face clocks for the towers of factories, churches and public buildings. He became the official clockmaker to the Great Northern, Midland and North Eastern Railway Companies.

Memorial to John Fowler (1826-64), inventor of the steam plough. This bronze model of his three-furrow balance plough formerly stood on a granite plinth in South Park, before disappearing in the 1970s, possibly rolled into the lake by vandals. The reversible, multiple ploughshares were hauled back-and-forth by wire rope between a pair of steam winch engines. 1856 was the year in which the first set was built. In 1860 Fowler founded the Fowler Engine Works in Leeds. This Quaker engineer and inventor married Joseph Pease's daughter Lucy.

Fowler steam roller. This Fowler engine is preserved in the public park next to the President's house and grounds in Funchal, Madeira.

Above: Great Burdon Mill. The Skerne and mill are on the left, the house and stable, or byre, are on the right.

Left: Great Burdon Mill interior, showing the miller's scales. A sack of grain would fit on the framed semicircle on the left, counterbalanced by the double scalepans on the right, with large weights on the lower and small weights on the upper.

Opposite, below: Darchem, 1964. Darlington Chemical & Insulating Co. Ltd, seen from West Auckland Road. The firm used the local dolomite to extract magnesia, leaving calcium carbonate as large hillocks of waste which attract lime-loving wild plants. The factory has been demolished and the area is now being landscaped as the new West Park housing development.

Darlington livestock market, 1964. The cattle market was laid out beside Bank Top station in 1878 between Park Lane and Clifton Street. At that time farm stock would be transported by railway cattle trucks. The auction market is alongside.

Pease's Low Mill, 1965. This stylish brick watermill was built in 1812 on the east bank of the Skerne opposite the Leadyard and was extended in 1818. It was reached from the town centre by a footbridge. In the early nineteenth century optical glass was made there. Steam power was soon adopted, serving in turn Pease's worsted mill, and George Denham's iron and brass foundry. The inner ring road, St Cuthbert's Way, built from 1963-73, now covers the site, but there is still a footbridge over the Skerne here beyond the new Town Hall grounds.

Pease's Mill, Crown Street, 1974. Viewed here from the inner ring road is the spinning mill and on the left, with a clock above the roof, are the offices. This town centre riverside site became a car park. Upstream were the weaving sheds at Railway Mill.

WRITE AT ONCE TO **HENRY PEASE & CO.'S** Successors

THE MILLS, DARLINGTON,

FOR PATTERNS OF THEIR NEW WINTER

DRESS FABRICS

Sent Post Free on Approval to any Address. Any Length Cut at Mill Prices.

All the Latest and most Fashionable Designs and entirely New Weavings of their World-renowned Gold Medal Merinos and Cashmeres, Cross-Warp Serges, and Rough and Ready Tweeds. New shades for the Season in charming variety.

Any article not approved exchanged within seven days. All Goods are warranted to be equal to Sample. Carriage Paid on all orders to any Railway Station in Great Britain, and to Dublin, Belfast, Limerick, Cork and Waterford.

London Sale Room: 244 REGENT ST. Over Jeff & Harris, the Furriers.

Where a full range of Patterns, as well as Goods in the piece, and finished Costumes, may be seen. Experienced Assistants are in attendance to take measurements and instructions for Dressmaking, and prompt execution of all orders is guaranteed.

Above: A Pease & Co. advertisement in the *Boys' Own Paper* dated January 1892 announces 'Merinos', 'Cross-Warp Serges' and 'Rough and Ready Tweeds'. Nuns' veiling was also made.

Opposite, below: The Skerne viewed northward from Victoria Bridge, 1964. The river in this area is now partly culverted and the inner ring road runs along the sites of the mills. Even the Haughton Road power station and cooling towers have gone and nowadays you can walk beside overhanging willows and watch mallard splashing about.

The main doorway of Darlington Locomotive Works, 1973. For a century from 1863, North Road Shops was to build, repair and overhaul engines for the North Eastern Railway Company. On its twenty-seven acre site it became the town's largest works, employing nearly 3,500 men. After the Beeching closures the erecting shops became a supermarket and North Road station became the Railway Centre and Museum.

North Road Shops rear yard, 1973. A separate siding opposite the entrance to North Road station was nicknamed 'the graveyard'. Engines waited here to be dismantled!

'Locomotion No.1', which powered the Stockton and Darlington Railway in 1825, was displayed on a plinth outside North Road station from 1857 until 1892 when it was moved to the interior of Bank Top station. When North Road Station Railway Museum was opened it was moved there. This postcard calls it 'No.1. Engine or Puffing Billy'.

Stockton and Darlington Railway stone sleepers preserved in South Park. From 1841 wooden sleepers replaced stone blocks.

'Locomotion No.1' when at Bank Top station platform, *c.* 1960.

'Derwent' at Bank Top station platform, *c.* 1960. Designed by Timothy Hackworth and built by W. and Alfred Kitching in 1845, it had oak plug wheels invented by Hackworth which reduced frost damage and improved reliability.

Bank Top station, Victoria Road, designed by William Bell and built in 1887. This is a Grade II listed building. Next to it, is the Grampian public house.

The North Eastern Hotel. Built at Pensbury Street corner on Victoria Road, it was convenient for the station entrance. It has been renamed the Coachman since this photograph was taken.

London & North East Railway east coast main line and sidings, Darlington. An atmospheric view looking south-eastward. The tower of St John's, the railwayman's church at Bank Top, rises above the smoky mist. *(Photograph by G.R. Jackson.)*

British Rail east coast main line viewed from Haughton Road Bridge, *c.* 1963. St John's church tower is on the left. Bank Top Station's clock tower is on the right (see page 91). Parkgate road bridge crosses over the railway lines.

THE
**CLEVELAND
BRIDGE**
AND
ENGINEERING Co.
LIMITED.

DARLINGTON
ENGLAND

Cleveland Bridge & Engineering Co. Ltd. The firm began in 1877 by buying the Skerne Works and took the fuller title in 1883. This cover picture of its 1930s brochure features their Lower Zambesi Bridge. Worldwide growth of railways entailed a need for strong bridges, at first of heavy steel. The motor age brought spectacularly graceful suspension bridges of breathtaking lengths.

Cleveland Bridge's construction yard, 1963, between Neasham Road and the main line. Early works included the Edward VII Tyne Bridge, Tweed Bridge, Victoria Falls Bridge, White Nile Bridge, the Blue Nile Bridge in 1909, bridges in Siam, Egypt, Queensland, Brazil, South Africa, New Zealand and China. After the Second World War it diversified into hangars, Bailey bridges, Mulberry floating harbours and post-war power stations. From the 1950s came large suspension bridges such as the Tamar Bridge near Plymouth in 1961 and the Forth Bridge, Severn Bridge and Humber Bridge, often built jointly with other firms.

Left: Bosporus Bridge. The first Bosporus Bridge in Turkey opened in 1973. It was the first ever land link between Europe and Asia. After being involved with the Forth Bridge 1964, the Severn Bridge and the Quebec Bridge, the firm introduced aerial spinning of the cables, and teamed up with UK steel contractors Sir Wm Arrol & Co. and future partners Dorman Long.

Below: Tsing Ma Bridge, Hong Kong. It was built to reach Chek Lap Kok airport on Lantau Island, the longest clear span bridge for combined road and railway in the world. It was built with an Anglo-Japanese consortium, with a five-year deadline before Hong Kong ownership passed from Britain to China in 1997.

Queen Elizabeth II Bridge, Dartford, east London, opened in 1973. Commonly known as the Dartford Crossing, it carries the M25 over the Thames estuary.

Thames Barrier, east London. Cleveland Bridge built and installed the flood gates and carried out site work, completed in 1982. Meanwhile the Cleveland Bridge & Engineering Co. moved from its Smithfield Road site to a greenfield site beside Yarm Road.

William Richardson & Co., horticultural and heating engineers. Their works at Smithfield Road founded in 1874 were later rebuilt and became well known to train passengers for the large thermometer standing beside the line. Richardson's made hot water heating systems for buildings and conservatories for landed gentry and city corporations as well as for owners of small villas throughout this country and abroad. Amdega continues the hardwood conservatory business from its site at Faverdale with both Richardson designs and new ones.

Haughton Hall conservatory. This was built on to the rear of the hall for J.M. While Esq.

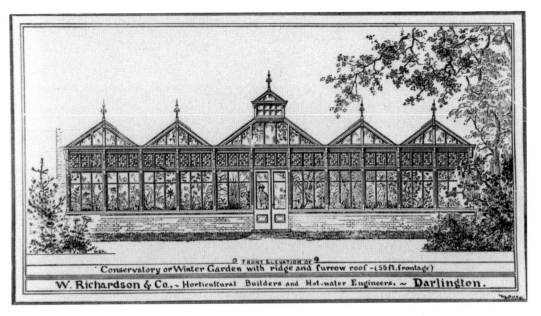

Design for a conservatory or winter garden with a ridge and furrow roof by W. Richardson & Co.

Preston Hall winter garden, 1883. It was built for Sir Robert Ropner (1838–1924), shipping merchant, coal exporter, shipbuilder, politician and philanthropist. He bought the Preston Hall estate near Stockton in 1881 as his home. The Richardson conservatory added in 1883 was rebuilt in 1998 and is part of a museum, art gallery and park developed from 1947 by Stockton Corporation.

Patons & Baldwins Ltd. The firm moved in 1947 from their cramped Clark Mills site in Halifax to this greenfield site at Darlington. Joined by their Scottish and Leicestershire workforce, it became the world's largest knitting yarn factory. Many different animal and man-made fibres were used to make the famous Beehive knitting yarns. The factory had a recreation centre on site, known as the Beehive Ballroom. *(Photograph courtesy of Aero Pictorial Ltd)*

Carding. The raw wool is sorted and blended, then washed to remove dirt and natural grease. The tufts of clean fibres are then carded into a continuous ribbon called sliver (as seen here). Forty-four carding machines are pictured here.

Spinning. After combing and dyeing, the sliver is drawn out between rollers, then spun or twisted into the required thickness (or 'count') and strength.

Reeling. Hanks of yarn are wound first into cones and then rewound (as seen here) into balls.

'Tiny Tim'. This gigantic steam hammer built in 1883 arrived in Beamish Park from Darlington Forge in 1977 to await restoration before becoming the now well-known entrance arch to Beamish North of England Open Air Museum. When the 15-ton hammer was in action, Darlington residents at nearby Albert Hill used to find their household crockery rattling, ornaments falling off mantelpieces, windows breaking and walls beginning to crack!

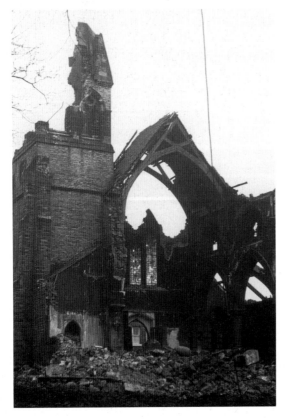

St Paul's church, North Road, Darlington. It was destroyed by fire on 26 November 1973, shortly before this photograph was taken, and had to be demolished. Built in 1868-70, to a severe Early English design of H.P. Pritchett junior, this was one of at least seventy new churches that he designed in the North East of England. He was also a designer of cemeteries, schools, offices, hotels and banks and undertook restorations.

seven

Events and Celebrations

Darlington bypass opening day. On 14 May 1966, this was the afternoon scene from Merrybent Bridge. The Co-op nurseries on the right grew soft fruits. The new road took the line of the disused Merrybent Railway which had served limestone quarries at Barton. Badgers were rescued before their setts were destroyed. The new road was later extended as the Durham motorway.

The frozen river Tees, Darlington. The scene is upstream from Broken Scar Dam on 22 December 1962. Rivers and waterfalls froze over like wedding cakes for three months, ending in a spectacular overnight thaw on 5-6 March 1963.

Darlington inner ring road, St Cuthbert's Way, built around 1970, seen from the end of the footbridge over the river Skerne which used to lead to Pease's Low Mill. In the distance is the Royal Mail Sorting Office and on the right is the bus station.

Darlington Borough Centenary Celebrations, 1967. A civic exhibition was mounted in the Baths Hall, Kendrew Street in which Darlington Historical Society, founded in 1961, assembled this Victorian period drawing room, using items lent by numerous members and local people.

Norman Sunderland. Darlington Historical Society, encouraged by Darlington Borough Council, also marked the centenary in 1967 by publishing Norman Sunderland's *A History of Darlington*. A leather-bound copy was presented to HM Queen Elizabeth II on her visit with the Duke of Edinburgh to the town's celebrations. *(Photograph courtesy of the Northern Echo.)*

Lady Cecilia Starmer. She came to Darlington in 1929 after marrying Sir Charles Starmer and supported all the good causes in the town. She was awarded the OBE in 1948, served as mayoress and was made a Freeman of the Borough in 1958, the first woman to receive this honour. Her special interests were the Operatic Society, the Memorial Hospital and two newly founded groups: Darlington Historical Society and the Friends of Darlington Civic Theatre. A delightful, unassuming person, much loved in the town, she died in December 1979, bequeathing Danby Lodge, house and grounds to Abbeyfield. *(Photograph of portrait courtesy of Abbeyfield.)*

Right: Darlington Museum, South Row, Market Place. The curator Alan Suddes says an official farewell to the author, lecturer and town guide Vera Chapman, the last visitor to the museum on its final closure at 5.30 pm on 31 March 1998. The collections were then dispersed.

Below: The first Civic Trust open days, on the weekend of 9 September 2001. They included a guided tour of the town centre, with an explanation of the burial wheel by the author.

The 150th Anniversary of the Stockton and Darlington Railway. A cavalcade of steam locomotives progressed from Shildon to Darlington on 27 September 1975. It was led by a replica of the original 'Locomotion No.1' driven by Mike Satow.

The Flying Scotsman, a 4-6-2 was followed by 910 NER a nineteenth-century 4-2-2 express locomotive to be housed in Darlington North Road Railway Museum.

A Tyne Tees Television crew filming the event.

NER 4-4-2 express locomotive.

Darlington and Teesdale Naturalists' Field Club, founded in 1891, on an outing.

Another early Field Club outing. Nothing strenuous, judging by the attire!

Above: Field Club Centenary, 1991.
Dr David Bellamy, the environmental
campaigner, led a nostalgic walk to the
Cow Green reservoir in Upper Teesdale,
the construction of which had initially
threatened the internationally famous
rare flora in the area. A pity about the
weather. Our birthday cake made by
his wife Rosemary was decorated with
little gentians made from blue icing.
Dr Bellamy has been a good friend to
the Club over the years, and referred
to it when he inaugurated the Skerne
Restoration Project.

Right: The black poplar. There was a
nationwide search in 1993 for surviving
specimens of the rare native black poplar
(*Populus nigra betufolia*). Several have now
been found in Darlington. Their branches
characteristically droop, but at their ends
turn dramatically upwards. They tend to
grow close to watercourses.

The Skerne Restoration. Serious river flooding nationally has led to research for control. Should rivers be canalised as was done at Blackwell, Barmpton and Ketton, or allowed to meander naturally, to spread and to reduce their speed? Restoration has been tried on the Brede in Denmark and the Cole in Wiltshire. David Bellamy inaugurated the Skerne Restoration Project in 1995. Since then the Field Club has reported a substantial increase in flora and fauna on the banks of the newly reinstated meanders as seen here in 2004.

The Skerne Restoration Bridge. This enables a circular walk through parkland using both sides of the river. The bridge 'chimney' echoes that of 'Locomotion No.1'. In the background is the embankment of the east coast main railway line, first built in 1844 for the Newcastle and Darlington Junction Railway.

Ladies on stilts during the Lantern Parade, 22 November 2001. In recent years an evening lantern parade has been revived following a route from the Arts Centre in Vane Terrace via Duke Street to the Market Place.

The 'fish lantern' and admirers.

Market Place refurbishment. Crowds are arriving for the opening celebrations on Sunday 14 April 1996. The Market Place had been repaved with Shap granite, an historic connection with erratic boulders deposited in the district at the end of the Ice Age and also with the massive Shap granite steps on High Row which were part of a late Victorian refurbishment.

The Bishop of Jarrow conducts the official opening ceremony.

The band plays in the locomotion wheel circle where thirty-two medieval Darlingtonians had been reburied after the archaeological excavation.

Old Darlington crafts and industries were demonstrated: farming, by a 'bull run', straw bales, sheaves and thatch.

Above: Brian Russell of Little Newsham forge demonstrates iron work.

Left: Leatherwork provided footwear, saddles and bridles.

Opposite above: The bishop, mayor and macebearer recess to the Town Hall.

Opposite below: The mounted police keep watch outside the Dolphin Centre during the reopening.

Left: Darlington by the Sea. A poster on Friday 23 July 2004.

Below: The temporary beach outside St Cuthbert's church gates.

Punch and Judy near the Boot and Shoe pub.

All the fun of the fair beneath the newly re-glazed canopy of the Covered Market. Note the bumpy granite setts to slow down what traffic is allowed.

The Mayor of Darlington, Councillor Frank Robson and the Bishop of Jarrow.

eight

Looking
Forward

Left: A new ornamental lamp. On the corner of Brinkburn's former stables built in 1862, now the offices of builders firm Estill Cooper, is this ornate lamp. Ornamental ironwork is becoming fashionable again, as well as being practical, especially as strong railings and gates. Such work by Brian Russell of Little Newsham forge, near Winston, is spreading around the Darlington area. Examples can easily be seen at the entrances to the Woodlands development on Milbank Road and around the Joseph Pease statue's plinth on High Row (see page 114).

Below: Victoria Embankment conservation area. This was designated in 1990 as 'an area of special architectural or historic interest whose character should be preserved or enhanced'. It includes the houses, road, river Skerne, its banks and Polam Bridge. The 1870s terraced houses reflect the course of the Skerne artificially channelled here in 1872, as do the paired mature lime trees on its banks. The iron post and chain rails on the right were previously on High Row.

South Park, Park House, swags and lake in 1905. Swags and medallions have continued through the ensuing years, but boating is a thing of the past. Some mature trees have had to be felled.

The Tea House, South Park, 1908. Under the South Park Restoration Project, the Tea House is to be restored, keeping the same log-built style. There will be a new educational and group visits centre between Park House and the café where teas and meals will be served.

New Town Hall and 'Resurgence'. The new Town Hall was opened by HRH Princess Anne, the Princess Royal, on 27 May 1970. On the site of the twelfth-century palace or manor house of Bishop de Puiset, the new Town Hall has offices of grey curtain walling linked to a separate luxurious council chamber by a soaring foyer in white marble. The metal sculpture 'Resurgence' by John Hoskins was a gift from Darlington Lions Club to celebrate the town's recovery after the closure of its railway industries in the 1960s.

Opposite, above: The Dolphin Centre. Opened in 1983 by Sir Roger Bannister CBE, this sports and leisure centre was designed by Gabriel Lowes, Borough Architect, on the site of the deanery and the old Dolphin Inn.

Opposite, below: The Cornmill Centre, Tubwell Row. A large shopping centre, it stands on the site of Darlington Co-op's department store. It was opened on 27 August 1992 by the Mayor of Darlington, Councillor David Lyonette, Mayoress Carol Lyonette and John Bywater, managing director of Burton Property Trust.

The supermarket at Morton Park opened in 1995. On the interior walls hang large photographs from the Ken Hoole Collection housed at Darlington Railway Museum. They show men at work in the local railway workshops and have been reproduced by permission of the Arts, Libraries and Museums Department of Durham County Council.

The New Darlington Memorial Hospital. Opened by HRH the Duchess of Kent on 22 May 1980, it dwarfs the original Memorial Hospital to which it is attached.

The former Reynolds Arena in 2004, now the Williamson Motors Stadium. This new football ground at the end of Neasham Road and beside the Darlington bypass opened at its new site in 2004 substantially financed for Darlington Football Club by George Reynolds. It supersedes the old ground at Feethams and has been renamed after its new sponsor.

'Train', a sculpture by David Mach, was unveiled by Lord Palumbo of Walbrook on 23 June 1997. Commissioned by Wm Morrison Supermarkets PLC and Darlington Borough Council and supported by the National Lottery through the Arts Council of England, it contains approximately 185,000 bricks. It can be viewed from a lay-by beside the bypass and visited on foot from Morrison's car park.

Northgate House. Initially named Telegraph House, this sole high-rise building in Darlington is an office block completed in 1977. Slow to let, it was not fully occupied until 1989. Renamed Northgate House, the top floor opened in 2003 as the aptly named Viewpoint Suite for conferences and training courses.

Vases on High Row. For over a century these vases, along with balustrading and great granite steps, have run the length of High Row. In three parallel levels they link the major architectural landmarks of Barclays Bank, the Town Clock, the Covered Market and old Town Hall, thus forming an integral part of a harmonious streetscape. But the view ahead is of a two-level arrangement, almost wholly pedestrianised, without the familiar ornaments. Many objections have been raised but the decision to go ahead had just been made at the time of writing.

Acknowledgements

This album is based on a selection of photographs I have taken and drawings made since coming to live in Darlington, supplemented by photographs from local institutions, businesses and private people. I have taken care to establish ownership and copyright, and apologise for any omissions or errors.

My sincere thanks go to those who kindly allowed me to copy their old photographs or to take photographs on their premises, and who gave me valuable information.

I would especially like to mention: Mrs Appleton, Elizabeth Armstrong, Moira Beswick, Mr Blakeway, Ken Chapman, Revd Philip Clark, Tony Cooper, Mrs D.A. Danby, John Fell, Ernie France, Betty Gaunt, Jim Gordon, Phyllis Hornsey, Ann Harrison, Mike Hein-Hartmann, Cassy Harker, Mr Jones, Mrs McKenzie, Ken McKeown, Chris Lloyd, Don Manson, Darren Naisbitt, Brian Notarianni, Paul Place, Mrs B. Simpson, Peter Tate, Bernice Walker, Steve Wright, Ms E. Yates, Amy Yeomans.

Thanks also go to: Amdega, Blackwell Grange Hotel, Cleveland Bridge, New Grange Hotel, Northgate House, St Teresa's Hospice.

Other local titles published by Tempus

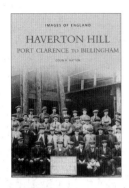

Haverton Hill: Port Clarence to Billingham
COLIN H. HATTON

This book tells the story of three communities that made up an industrial area covering the north bank of the River Tees, from the coming of the Stockton & Darlington Railway, through the growth of the steel and chemical industries, to the decline of Teeside's engineering industry over the last thirty years. With old photographs and reminiscences of local residents, it provides a fascinating record of everyday life in these close-knit communities.

0 7524 3425 X

Around Grangetown
JOHN M. O'NEILL

With over 200 images, this volume features some of the important events and developments that have taken place in this area from Victorian times to the 1950s. It describes the impact of the iron and steelworks, which brought employment to the area, the effects of war on the community, and provides a unique pictorial history of aspects of everyday life, in schools, churches, pubs, shops and streets.

0 7524 3282 6

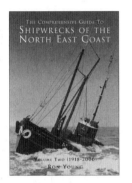

Shipwrecks of the North-East Coast
Volume II (1918-2000)
RON YOUNG

In this second volume, from the last years of the Second World War to the end of the twentieth century, Ron Young charts the history of the ships, boats, submarines and their crews, that were lost along the north-east coast from Berwick-on-Tweed to Whitby, and the brave lifeboat crews that went to their aid. This comprehensive guide is an absorbing companion volume to *Shipwrecks of the North East Coast – Volume One (1740 – 1917)*.

0 7524 1750 9

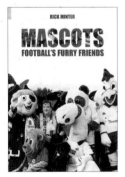

Mascots Football's Furry Friends
RICK MINTER

Follow the story of Cyril the Swan (the 8ft rascal at Swansea), relive the tale of H'Angus (Hartlepool's monkey mascot who got elected as mayor) and see the capers of Yorkie, the King of the Jungle who fought to save York City. See how Manchester United's Fred the Red is even busier than his manager! This remarkable guide reveals a crazy and colourful world of glamour, fun and rivalry, with profiles of characters in the Premiership, Football League, Scotland and beyond.

0 7524 3179 X

If you are interested in purchasing other books published by Tempus, or in case you have difficulty finding any Tempus books in your local bookshop, you can also place orders directly through our website

www.tempus-publishing.com